CONTENTS

PAGE

Other Large Print Books
published by
Christian Focus Publications

J. C Ryle	Assurance
Barbara Honour	Gems From Genesis
Charles H. Spurgeon	God Always Cares
Francis Ridley Havergal	Starlight Through The Shadows
F. B. Meyer	Peace Perfect Peace

God   Can
Be   Trusted

George   Muller

Christian   Focus   Publications   Ltd.

Published by
Christian Focus Publications Ltd.
Geanies House, Fearn, Ross-shire,
IV20 1TW, Scotland, Great Britain

First printed 1990
Reprinted 1993

1. THE GOD Of JESHURUN

(Deuteronomy 33:26-29)

There is none like unto the God of Jeshurun, who rideth upon the heavens in thy help, and His excellency on the sky.

This portion, is connected with the blessing which Moses gave to the various tribes of Israel, just before the Lord took him away. After giving a particular blessing to each one of the tribes, the blessing in these verses is now uttered, by the Spirit speaking through the prophet, with regard to all the tribes of Israel. The Holy Spirit sums up all the previous blessings in this last which He begins by the words, "There is none like unto the God of Jeshurun."

Imputed righteousness

Jeshurun means, "the righteous," or "the righteous one." And this is one of the titles given to the Israelites. Strange title, is it not to be given by the Spirit to that stiff-necked people, who had again and again provoked the God of Israel, and who had sinned against Him times without number? Stiff-necked and rebellious though they had been, yet they are here called "the righteous." In speaking of this people, the

Holy One calls them "right-eous."

Precisely so is it with ourselves - by nature we are sinners, and great sinners; and not only so, but deserving punishment, and nothing but punishment; yet the moment a poor sinner is brought to believe on the Lord Jesus Christ he is called righteous. "We are all by nature children of wrath, even as others," yet by faith in the Lord Jesus Christ we are accepted, regenerated - that is, born again; instead of the children of wrath, we become the children of God, we are brought out of darkness into His marvellous light, are delivered from the powers of darkness, and translated into the kingdom of His dear Son- are brought on the road to heaven, and have before us the bright and blessed prospect of our Father's house.

Saved by grace through faith

Through faith in the Lord Jesus Christ, these and all other blessings of the gospel become ours. Fear is lost, judgement is taken away, and instead of all that, we instantaneously become children of God.

Instantaneously we obtain the

forgiveness of our sins, are made alive in Christ Jesus, and are "delivered from the powers of darkness, and translated into the kingdom of His dear Son." But this is only obtained by faith in the Lord Jesus Christ.

Oh, glorious gospel that we should be called the sons of God! When we look inward, we see that we are utterly unworthy of such honour - we can indeed see we are anything but righteous. Yet we are called "righteous," and are united to the Lord Jesus Christ, and partake by faith of His perfect righteousness.

Now, regarding these Israelites, it is here stated that "There is none like unto the God of Jeshurun." There is no god like unto their God. They had the living God, while others had but dead idols.

The Lord our portion

And this is especially our portion: we have the God and Father of our Lord Jesus Christ to be our God and Father. That is, we have the living God on our side, to be our God, our Guide, our Father, and our Friend. All this, however, is only true of us if we believe in the Lord Jesus Christ. We may speak about Him as our God; we may read about Him; we may be able to explain certain passages of Scripture concerning Him; we may even have written much about Him; and may have preached in His name; and yet it may not be true of us that we have the living God for our Father, except we really believe in the Lord Jesus Christ, and trust in Him alone for the salvation of our souls.

But if we do thus accept Jesus as our Saviour, then it is true of us that we have God as our Father, and we have the same precious share in those blessings as the literal Israelites had. It can be said of us, "There is none like unto the God of Jeshurun."

The Lord our strength

But further, with regard to these blessed ones, it is said, *"Who rideth upon the heavens in thy help and His excellency on the sky ."* Look at this expression, "Rideth upon the heavens in thy help." Such a thought as this would never have entered into the mind of the greatest poet who ever lived, except he had borrowed it from the Bible. All the best and noblest ideas in the poets they have borrowed from that source. The thought here is that there is none who can resist God - that no power on earth can oppose Him. The powers of this earth - that is, all under heaven - are as nothing before Him. He is the Creator - they are the creatures, and they cannot withstand Him, who is above all.

The Lord our deliverer

Now, the comfort to us is that we have such a God for our helper - one who rides on the heavens - in the very sky; we have Him to fight on our behalf. He is above all, He is out of the reach of Satan and wicked men, He cannot be defeated by any of them. He is above the elements, and they cannot withstand Him, neither can any creature stand against Him, who is the chiefest of all. He is on our side, He is for us, and if God be for us who can be against us? If He is on our side all is well with us. But, alas! if He is against us, what shall become of us? If we are in Him we are in perfect safety.

But if there be anyone reading this book who has not God on his side, who has never believed on the Lord Jesus Christ, let me implore you, be you reconciled -

be you at peace with God. If so, then you will be safe, and then it will be said with regard to you, that "He rideth upon the heavens in your help." All that we have to do, feeling as we must our own weakness, impotency, and helplessness, is but to cast ourselves into His arms, and say, "My Father, I am Thy child, Thy poor, weak, helpless child; be nigh unto me, and help me."

What will our Father, who rides upon the heavens, do? Most assuredly, He will assist His poor weak child. Whatever his necessities may be, he may feel assured that the everlasting arms are around him, and that his Father will thrust out the enemies, and will destroy them utterly.

Trying circumstances

Remember, that when this blessing was given, the Israelites had not yet entered the promised land, although on the point of doing so. Moreover, even if they had crossed the Jordan, there were still the seven mighty nations of the Canaanites to be overcome; and therefore at such a time they needed the help of the living God, and were blessed by being reminded that they had such a helper.

And so with us, the Israel of God, and the heirs of the promise. We have much conflict yet before us, and so these words are for our encouragement. God, the living God, is our refuge. As if the Holy Spirit by the prophet would say, "True, you have these great and mighty enemies to overcome, but in going forward, remember that God will be at your side as your helper. Commit yourselves to Him, look to Him, trust in Him, depend on Him and you will find the power of His mighty arm will save you." What

He would have us remember and take courage in is the fact that *the eternal God is our refuge.* Can we, each one of us, say this, "God, the eternal, living God, is my refuge"? For myself, I can say He is my only refuge, and has been so for fifty years. How many of you can say the same? Ask yourselves individually this deeply important question. If you are able to say this with regard to yourselves, what a happy people you are. But if not able to say it, yet there is no reason why you should not be able to say it. It is only trust in Him that is required; nothing else but to place yourselves wholly in His hands. If you will only depend on the Lord Jesus Christ for the salvation of your souls, it may be yours now. Just as it is true of me, a poor, miserable sinner, and true of many thousands who, like me, are poor miserable sinners, but who now trust in Him, so it may be true of you, that there is none like your God, who rideth upon the heaven in your help.

The eternal God

But further, "*the eternal God is thy refuge, and underneath are the everlasting arms.*" There is something peculiarly sweet to me to have an eternal Friend, a living Friend, a Friend who is above all, who has all power and might, and that He is on my side.

It is well indeed to have an earthly friend, who, if you are in poverty, may help you. But sickness may come, he may be taken away by death; or, if not that, he may lose all his wealth with which he helped you, and thus may be unable further to assist you. But none of these things affect the living God - He is the same yesterday, to-day, and for ever. Eternal is thy refuge. Fifty years ago He was as now; a thousand years ago - ten thousand years ago - He is ever the same.

The God of Elijah is here to-day, and He is exactly the same as He was in the prophet's time - as ready and as willing to help His children. The living God is with us, whose power never fails, whose arm never grows weary, whose wisdom is infinite, and whose power is unchanging. Therefore to-day, to-morrow, and next month, as long as life is continued, He will be our helper and friend.

Still more, even as He is through all time, so will He be

through all eternity. Oh, the blessedness of having the eternal God on our side! Not only on our side, but on whom we may rely as on a fortress of strength, in whom we may get refuge continually, and in whom there is perfect security.

False views of Christianity

If the world only knew the blessedness of thus having God as our refuge, I think the whole world would seek at once after the Lord. It is only because they think it is something miserable to be a Christian, and do not know that it is infinitely more precious to be a Christian than to be without God, that they are content to remain unsaved.

This is one great reason why they do not seek to enjoy the things of God. And it is just the reason why you and I should make it our business to be out-and-out Christians, that we may show to the world what it is to be truly happy Christians, and at the same time be living examples to the Church. But this true and real joy cannot be possessed unless we are out-and-out Christians. There must not be a seeking to hold fast the things of the world to the utmost, and yet seeking to get to heaven all the same. If this be the case with us, we shall just have enough religion to make us miserable, and too little to make us happy.

What does God want

That we should be happy Christians; and this we can only be if we are holy Christians. We shall never, of course, be altogether free from sin on this earth; not that until we are taken home. But we must aim after being holy children; we must not go on in what we know is contrary to the divine will. And if we are really out-and-out Christians, and are really holding on to the eternal living God, the result will be that we shall be happy Christians, and shall be bearing testimony to those "that are without."

And the result of this will be to stir them up to seek after the Lord; and so a thousand Christians will be a thousand witnesses for the living God. Therefore, my beloved brethren and sisters, let us lay it to heart to be out-and-out Christians, so that we may lay hold of this word - *the living God is thy refuge.*

I am a weak erring sinner, yet I

have the living God on my side, the eternal God as my refuge. Oh, the blessedness of having such a refuge as this. What are all earthly honours in comparison with this? What the highest dignities? What the greatest earthly crown as compared with the blessedness which we possess in having the living eternal God on our side, and of being permitted to make Him our refuge?

And this is the position of the child of God; above everything that man can conceive, "underneath are the everlasting arms," with the power of the almighty

God for our helper. What a comfort in our helplessness, to know that although you and I are weak, erring, and feeble naturally, and can do nothing if left to ourselves; yet we have these everlasting arms underneath us to support us. Though we are helpless, here is an almighty arm to lean upon, and even to lie upon. It is an arm that can carry us through the difficulties which lie before us, and through the trials which await us; can bear us safely through, can carry us in all our helplessness. Oh, the blessedness of the figure used here -

"The eternal God is thy refuge, and underneath are the everlasting arms!"

The Deliverer

Further, *"And He shall thrust out the enemy from before thee, and shall say, Destroy them."* What a blessed promise was this to the Israelites! Before them was the Jordan to be crossed; and even if it were crossed, were there not those great and mighty nations to be overcome? Looking to themselves, they might well have been afraid; but it must not be thus, there must be no fear in those underneath whom are the everlasting arms. Further to encourage them, Jehovah distinctly says with regard to these seven mighty nations, 'I will thrust out the enemy from before you, and will say, "Destroy them". '

Look at the entrance of the children of Israel, and see how this was fulfilled. Look at the crossing of the Jordan; see how the walls of Jericho fell. Look at the various battles with the enemy. When kings came against them, how easily they were overcome. When nations united against them, still Jehovah was on their side; and at last, all were thrust out and destroyed - overcome by the power of Jehovah.

Now, this is particularly comforting with regard to ourselves. We are a feeble band, a "little flock;" our enemies are mighty and strong. "We have no power in ourselves against this great army." So must we look on all this as a hopeless case, and exclaim, "We can never get to heaven; we are so weak, helpless, and sinful in ourselves?" Well, it is quite true, we are so weak and helpless in ourselves, that we cannot overcome those that are against us; but our Helper is

mighty, and though these enemies were ten thousand times
more numerous than they are,
and though they would easily
overcome us if faced in our own
power, yet it is still true that *Jehovah saves,* and that He has promised to thrust out the enemy from
before us, even to destroy them.
All the power of evil will not
finally prevail, though at times it
appears as if it would be so. Neither shall the corrupt nature
within us finally have the victory;
but through the Lord Jesus
Christ we shall have the victory,
and be more than conquerors.

Therefore, right blessed is the prospect before us! If we look at ourselves, there is abundant reason to be cast down. Yet we must never forget the word, that we shall have the victory through the Lord Jesus Christ, for "greater is He that is for us than all that can be against us," and through the God and Father of our Lord Jesus Christ we shall finally have the victory.

God's Deliverances

In the literal fulfilment of the promise with regard to the Israelites, the enemy was destroyed, but not at all through their own strength. It was solely by God helping them that these were destroyed. Remember how God fought for them time after time. How the sun stood still at the request of Joshua. How, again, the elements from heaven fought for them; how stones were hailed upon the enemy. The hornets also were by Jehovah used for the destruction of the enemies. In various ways Jehovah fought on their behalf, and showed His mighty power in leading His people to possess the land.

So now with the Israel of God;

they can of themselves do nothing, having nothing but weakness; but again and again God delivers them; so that while in this life they can never be perfectly delivered from the power of the enemy, yet they shall finally be helped by their God. Further,

"Israel then shall dwell in safety alone."

I wish you to mark this word, "alone," most particularly. It contains the idea of "separation"- safety in separation. "Israel then shall dwell in safety alone." The safety is dependent on their dwelling alone; the safety is dependent on their entire separation from other nations. It was to be their peculiar position of separateness from others: it was to be their very safety. God intended them to be separate, He forbade their entering into marriage with the other nations, or in any other way forming connections with them. They must destroy the surrounding nations and walk separately.

Now if my beloved brethren will walk according to the mind of God, that is what they must do - come out, and be separate. There must be separation from the world. Naturally, we are inclined to give up the line of demarcation, and to say, "This is too strict, too particular; why should I be so much separated from the world? See that brother, he is enjoying the world a little, he is mixing with the world, and so is able to make something of each world, and he is a Christian. Why should not I also be able to mix somewhat with the world, and yet get to heaven at last?"

Mark! mark! my beloved Christian friends. What the Lord requires is, that we should live *separate from the world.*

God Can Be Trusted

Of course, as our business is here, we must have something to do with the world, yet we should not go on in the spirit of the world. It is quite possible that we should conduct our business carefully, and yet be separate to the Lord. God does not see it good to take us out of the world. Jesus prayed with regard to us, "I pray not that Thou shouldest take them out of the world, but that Thou shouldest keep them from the evil." The apostle Paul says, "Come out from among them, and be ye separate." Thus, if we desire to attain nearness of communion with God, we must be willing to live in separation from the world, and to aim at a decided line of demarcation between the world and the Church, which will be for the praise, honour, and glory of God. This we cannot do if we are living as the world does, or seeking to be as much like the world as possible. In so doing we shall only bring dishonour upon the name of God, and misery upon ourselves. Beloved Christian friends, let us keep rank against the world, living in separation from its habits, maxims, and principles, and aim at conformity to the mind of the Lord Jesus Christ, rather than, as many seem to do, to try to live as much like the world as possible.

We ought to be a "Marked People"

Men should know that we are servants of the Lord Jesus Christ; even as our blessed Master Himself, who did not seek to be like the scribes and Pharisees, but rather sternly denounced them. He Himself said that "He must be about the business of His Father;" that was His grand object. And that is what we must aim after. In the business and matters of this life we must of necessity mix, to a certain extent, with the world, but we must, day by day, and hour by hour, seek to live as much as possible unlike the world. Thus only is it that we bring forth fruit abundantly to the praise, honour, and glory of the Lord.

I would ask you most affectionately, my beloved brethren and sisters, "Are you willing to be such disciples - such out-and-out Christians, and to be such children of God?" This, remember, is the kind of children that God looks for; such disciples the Lord

God Can Be Trusted

Jesus desires to have - men who are willing to live only for Him. Such children, such disciples, are certainly needed for these days. The eyes of the world are upon us, to see if we do live according to our profession. Surely, then, it is expected that we should live so that we may bring glory to God.

By thus living out-and-out for the Lord, we should become bolder and bolder. He will grant us more grace and more help, and we shall be delivered. "Thus Israel shall dwell in safety alone." Even so. And *"The fountain of Jacob shall be upon a land of corn and wine*." That means *fruit - fulness* - the fountain in the midst of a land of corn and wine. But in the Hebrew, the word here rendered "fountain" also means "eye," and therefore it means "the eye of Jacob shall be upon a land of corn and wine." The land into which the Israelites were to be brought, was to be a land of plenty, "a land flowing with milk and honey." When they entered the land, they did find abundance. So with reference to ourselves, having been brought into safety, we shall also be brought into a land of plenty. We shall be fed with the finest of the wheat, and with corn and wine, to strengthen and encourage in the work of the Lord.

"Also the heavens shall drop down dew ." We are to be brought into a fruitful country spiritually, in which there is no such thing as drought. The children of God have the promise that they shall be well watered, their soul shall delight itself in fatness.

"Happy art thou, O Israel; who is like unto thee, O people saved by the Lord, the shield of thy help, and who is the sword of thy excellency! and thine enemies

shall be found liars unto thee; and thou shalt tread upon their high places." This was spoken just as they were about to enter the land of promise.

"*Happy Art Thou, O Israel*" They were, it is true, about to enter the land, but before them they had the great and mighty nations. Now if this was true of the literal Israel, how far more abundantly ought it to be true regarding the Israel of God. Believers in the Lord Jesus Christ, is it true of you? "Happy art thou, O Israel."

I desire to give my testimony

that it is true of me. Though a poor miserable sinner, I am a very happy man. Though just now nearly seventy years of age, and though having been fifty years in the spiritual life, yet I have not grown unhappy; I am still very happy. Even as it is true of me, so it might be true of each of you. Why not? It is the will of our Lord Jesus Christ, that all His disciples should be happy disciples. Let us, then, aim after it. For there is such a thing as being holy and happy children - such a thing as being thoroughly decided Christians, and yet being happy. It is the will of the Father that we should be happy.

What is the reason that we are not all happy? Let each of you ask the question, and answer it before God to yourselves - "Why, why, why! am I not a happy child of God - a happy disciple of the Lord Jesus Christ?" There is nothing whatever to hinder us, so far as God's truth is concerned. God delights to see you all happy. Do not say, "Oh, Mr. Muller, if you had my trial, my burden, you could not be happy." What a mistake! The Christian may be ever a happy man. While the

world is dependent upon surrounding circumstances for ap-
parent happiness, the Christian
may be truly happy, whatever his
circumstances may be, so long as
he is really trusting in God, and
satisfied with Him.

Therefore, my beloved Christian friends

*Never Attempt to Carry Your
Own Burden,*

but learn to roll it upon the
Lord. Seek to deal with Him
about everything; if you have any
trial, any perplexity, cast it upon
Him. Then you will find out how
ready He is to help, and you will be

able to say, even in view of all these circumstances, "I am happy."

If we are unhappy, the fault lies with ourselves. There is no reason why we should not be happy children. Our Father loves us, and He will lead us safely through. Having such a Father, it may well be said of us, "Happy art thou, O Israel; who is like unto thee, O people saved by the Lord, the shield of thy help, and who is the sword of thy excellency."

These Israelites were happy because they had such a God. Look how He delivered them and saved them. It was He who delivered them from the Egyptians, who led them through the Red Sea, destroying the hosts of Pharaoh. It was He who led them through the wilderness, provided them with heavenly food, and water from the rock, and finally led them into the land of promise.

Cause for Happiness

And remember that it is by Him that you and I are delivered from a worse power than Egypt: are delivered from greater enemies than the host of the Egyptians and by Him we are led through the many difficulties of this life. Daily

He is leading us, until at length He will land us safely above. Ought we not then to be happy, truly happy in the Lord? I ask you, affectionately, is it so with you? Are you all happy Christians? You ought to be, if you will only look to Him. Trust Him with child-like simplicity, and you will see how ready He is to help you, and to give blessing.

2. THE SECRET OF PRE-VAILING PRAYER
(Acts 12:1-19)

I desire Christian friends, to bring before you, for encouragement in prayer, a precious instance in which an answer to united supplication is given.

"Now about that time Herod the king stretched forth his hands to vex certain of the church. And he killed James the brother of John with the sword.." James was the first apostle who became a martyr for Christ. Stephen had previously been stoned, but he was not an apostle.

Satan's Power Limited

"And because he saw it pleased the Jews, he proceeded further to take Peter also." Now Peter, indeed, seems to be at death's gate; but the Lord said, "Thus far shalt thou go, and no further." This we have to keep before us, that Satan, though he hates us, can go no further than the Lord gives him liberty.

The most striking instance of this, we find in the case of Job. Satan had tried to get at him but was unable to do so; and at last he has to make confession before the Lord, "Hast Thou not made a hedge about him, and about his house, and about all that he hath on every side?" Satan had tried to get at him, but by reason of the hedge he was unable to get at the person or substance of Job. It was only by the permission of God, and when this hedge was removed, that he was able to get at the substance of Job. And even still, the hedge was around the person of Job, and not until this hedge had been removed, was he able to touch the person of Job. Though we must never lose sight of the fact that on the one hand Satan may be, and often is, powerful to hurt us, yet on the other hand, He that is with us is more powerful still, and Satan can do nothing without the permission of the Lord.

"And when he had apprehended him, he put him in prison, and delivered him to four quaternions of soldiers to keep him." He was delivered to sixteen soldiers - four little companies of four soldiers each, who were to be responsible for him; so that there might be two inside, and two outside, and so always some to take care of him. Thus it seemed to be utterly impossible

that he could escape. *"Intending after Easter to bring him forth to the people."* It is called Easter, but there was no such thing as Easter then. It was the feast of unleavened bread.

"Peter, therefore, was kept in prison; but prayer was made without ceasing of the church unto God for him."

Here we have prayer in church capacity. The saints at Jerusalem meeting together, and giving themselves to prayer, and from what we see afterwards, it was *prayer without ceasing.* There was always some little band at prayer - *"prayer was made without ceasing of the church unto God for him."*

They did not say, Now we will send a petition to Herod to let him go. They might have sent in such a petition, for by this time there were thousands in Jerusalem who believed in the Lord Jesus Christ. They were a formidable company by that time; and if they had all written down their names to this petition they might have succeeded. And if thus they did not succeed, they might have raised a large sum of money. They were very willing to give of their substance, to sell their houses and lands for the poor of the church; and most certainly they would have willingly done so for the deliverance of Peter. They did not do this, though a most probable way of getting Peter delivered would have been to have bribed some of Herod's courtiers. Even in this very chapter we find that when disunion had arisen in regard to the men of Tyre and Sidon, some individuals bribed a courtier, the king's chamberlain, and thus made peace. Therefore it might possibly have succeeded if they had done so. But none of these things did they use; they gave themselves to prayer. And that, my beloved friends, is the best weapon they could have used. There is not a more blessed and powerful weapon for the children of God, than they should give themselves to prayer. For thus they can have the power of God on their side - the almighty power of God. And by making use of this power, through the instrumentality of prayer in all things we need, we can have the infinite wisdom of God brought to work for us, and have God Himself at our side, as children of God. Therefore we should seek to make a far better use than ever we have done of prayer. And you, my beloved Christian friends, who are in the habit of meeting often at the prayer meeting, expect great things at the hands of God; look out for wondrous blessings, and you will find how ready He is to give those things which we ask for. This, then, these saints at Jerusalem did - they gave themselves to prayer without ceasing. That is, they believed that though Herod had apprehended Peter for the purpose of slaying him, and though this Herod was a notoriously wicked man, as we all know, yet God was able to deliver him from this blood-thirsty Herod. They believed that nothing was too hard for God to accomplish, and therefore they prayed without ceasing.

Waiting for the Answer

Now, notice, we do not know how long Peter was in prison, but it is an obvious and natural inference that he had been apprehended before those days of unleavened bread; as after these days his execution was to take place, and, therefore, at least he was in prison seven days. Now, it was not on the first day that the prayer was answered. They met together and prayed, - prayed earnestly; but the first day, hour by hour, passed away, and yet Peter was in prison. The second day, and again they are found waiting on God in prayer. Still, hour by hour, the second day passed, and yet he was not delivered. And so the third, and fourth, and fifth days passed away. They are still waiting on God; prayer is made without ceasing; yet this holy man remained in prison; and there seemed to be no prospect of

God answering their prayers.

And thus, beloved friends, you and I shall find again and again that the answer is delayed; and the question is, shall we give up praying, or shall we continue? The temptation is to cease praying, as though we had given up hope, and to say, "It is useless; we have already prayed so long that it is useless to continue." This is just what Satan would have us say; but let us persevere and go on steadily praying, and be assured that God is both able and willing to do it for us; and that it is the very joy and delight of His heart, for

Christ's sake, to give to us all things which are for the glory of His name, and our good and profit. If we do so, He will give us our desire. As assuredly as we are the children of God, if we pray perseveringly, and in faith, the prayer will be answered. Thus let us learn from this precious instance regarding prayer, which the Holy Ghost has given for our encouragement.

"And when Herod would have brought him forth, the same night Peter was sleeping between two soldiers, bound with two chains, and the keepers before the door."

Mark, that the last night before his execution is now come, and yet Peter is asleep. Not carelessly and indifferently was he lying there, but calmly, quietly resting in the arms of Jesus, and leaning on the bosom of his Lord. He is bound with two chains, as the custom was, between two soldiers, one on the one side and one on the other side, that he might not escape.

God's Manner of Answering the Prayer

And now the deliverence; we will see in what way God works.

"And behold, the angel of the

Lord came upon him, and a light shined in the prison." We should have said, this must be done in the dark, and as quietly as possible. But see, the light came into the prison. Humanly speaking, this would have wakened the soldiers; but not thus with Jehovah; when He works, He can do His will, notwithstanding all these things.

The angel "*smote Peter on the side and raised him up, saying, Arise up quickly,*" without any fear that in addressing Peter the soldiers should be wakened.

"*And as he rose, the chains fell from off his hands.*" Still there was no fear of arousing the soldiers.

"Gird thyself." There is no need to hurry; he is to be taken out, but is to dress himself properly.

And now comes the strangest thing of all, *Bind on thy sandals* . These wooden shoes must be bound on the feet. We should have said, let him walk out without them, that no noise be made to awaken the sleeping soldiers. Not thus; it was God who wrought the deliverance, and when He works there is no need to fear, for who can withstand?

God Can Be Trusted

And so he did. And the angel saith unto him, *"Cast thy garment about thee."* His outer garment is to be put on. Everything, therefore, is to be done in an orderly manner. It is as if Herod had sent a messenger to deliver him; he is to go quietly forth.

"When they were past the firstt and second ward." The eyes of the keepers were miraculously shut.

But now they come to *"the iron gate."* Many, many times do we come to some such iron gate. He was now out of the prison, and past the soldiers who were watching, but now he comes to this great iron gate. How shall he get out of prison after all? And so it is with you and me at times. Everything seems prepared, and difficulties have been removed; and yet, after all, there seems to be one great obstacle which is insurmountable. Can we escape? Yes! God is able to open the iron gate for you and for me, even as He caused the great iron gate of the prison to open of its own accord. Let us expect everything from God, and He will do it, if it is for His glory, and our good and profit.

God Can Be Trusted

God's Unchangeable Power

But can He do miraculous things today? Yes, as well as He could in the middle of the first century. Let us never say this was in the days of the apostles, and we cannot expect such things now. Quite true, that God does not commonly work miracles; but He can if He will, and let us give glory to His name, that if He does not work miracles it is because He can and does do His will by ordinary means. He can accomplish His ends in many ways. Let us never lose heart in such circumstances; He has the same power as ever He had. Many think if they were living in the days of Elijah, or in the days of Elisha or in the days of the apostles, they would expect these things; but because they do not live in those days, therefore they cannot expect to have such answers to prayer. This is wrong; remember, that God has the same power as in the days of the prophets of old, or of the apostles of old; therefore let us only look for great blessings, and great blessings will be bestowed on us, my beloved friends in Christ.

"They passed through one street, and forthwith the angel

departed from him." This contains an important spiritual truth -
it is this, that God does not work
miracles when they are not
needed. The angel was sent to
deliver Peter from prison; but
Peter was now in the streets, and
he knew very well the streets of
Jerusalem. He had been living
there, and he knew all about
them; and it was not, therefore,
necessary that the angel should
lead him through the streets, and
bring him to the house where he
was going. Therefore as soon as
he was outside the prison, and no
more supernatural help was re-

quired, the angel departed from him.

The Deliverance Effected

"And when Peter was come to himself, he said, Now I know of a surety that the Lord hath sent His angel, and hath delivered me out of the hands of Herod, and from all the expectation of the people of the Jews." He wist not that it was true at first, and thought that it must be a vision, but now that he finds himself in the streets, he knows that God has indeed delivered him.

"And when he had considered the thing, he came to the house of

Mary the mother of John, whose surname was Mark, where many were gathered together praying." Notice this, "many were gathered praying." For what purpose? For Peter's deliverance unquestionably; because prayer was made by the church on his behalf without ceasing. Though it was the night before his execution, they did not lose heart. To the eye of man the case seems hopeless, but they still came together to pray. Therefore they had not only begun well, but they had also gone on well; they had continued in prayer.

"And as Peter knocked at the

door of the gate, a damsel came to hearken, named Rhoda. " Her name is given. Why so? When this was written down, inquiry might be made as to the truth of the account. The damsel, probably, was then living, and thus opportunity for this inquiry was afforded.

"And when she knew Peter's voice, she opened not the gate for gladness, but ran in and told how Peter stood before the gate." Here we find a description so true to life. What shall we say? The damsel heard his voice and knew it; she knew they were praying for

Peter's deliverance; her heart was so glad that first of all she runs to tell that Peter stood at the door. She could not open the door. Now what do we expect to hear out of the mouths of those beloved brethren in Christ, those holy men who have been waiting upon God day after day? Surely it will be praise.

Failing Faith

Ah! there it is which shows what we are. *"Thou art mad ."* I specially seek, in bringing this before you, that we may learn what we are naturally. They had begun well, and had gone on well, yet failed completely in the end. They had faith at the first, and exercised faith, but had no faith in the end. Let us be warned, beloved friends; that is just what we must seek to avoid. It is comparatively easy for us to begin well and to go on well, day after day, week after week, month after month; but it is difficult to remain faithful to the end. Even thus it was regarding those of whom we are ready to say, "we are not worthy to unloose their shoes"; and if they failed, what of us? What say they? "Thou art mad." They are praying for the thing, and it comes; yet this is what they say. Those men had begun in faith, had gone on in faith, and yet it is gone. They had continued outwardly to wait upon God, but at last without expectation. If they had continued in faith, they would have said, when they heard the tidings, "Blessed be God; let His holy name be praised!" I am as certain of this as though an audible voice had told me from heaven. It would have been impossible for them to say to Rhoda "Thou art mad," when she brought the news of Peter's freedom, unless faith had been gone.

*If we Ask let us be Looking
for the Answer*

*"But she constantly affirmed
that it was even so. Then said
they, It is his angel. But Peter
continued knocking; and when
they had opened the door, and
saw him, they were astonished. "*
Another proof that they were
wanting in faith at that time,
"they were astonished." True
faith is thus known, that when we
begin in faith, and continue in
faith, we are not astonished when
the answer comes. For instance,
suppose any of you have beloved
sons or daughters who are un-

converted for whom you have been praying long. At last they have been brought to the Lord. The test, whether you have been praying in faith or not, is, if you say, " The Lord be praised for it," and you receive the tidings gladly; then you have been exercising faith.

If I may use a phrase in the right sense, "We take it as a matter of course." So, in a spiritual sense, we should be so confident that God will bless, and that He will answer what we ask, that when it comes, we should still be so confident as to say, "We take it as a matter of course; it could not be otherwise; the thing must come because God has pledged to give the blessing."

"But he, beckoning unto them with the hand to hold their peace, declared unto them how the Lord had brought him out of prison. And he said, Go show these things unto James and to the brethren; and he departed, and went into another place."